Absence of Unicorns,
Presence of Lions

Other publications by the same author

Poetry
The Cost of Living, 1957
A Book of Pictures, 1962

Novels
The Notebooks of Susan Berry, 1963
Helmet and Wasps, 1966.

Children's novels
Master Entrick, 1966
The Blind Cross, 1969.

Absence of Unicorns, Presence of Lions

Poems by Michael Mott

For Larry ~ best wishes at St. Mary's
December 10th 1983
Michael
Michael Mott

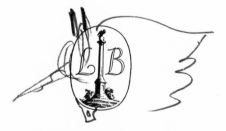

Little, Brown and Company
Boston/Toronto

FIRST EDITION
02/76

Library of Congress Cataloging in Publication Data
Mott, Michael.
Absence of unicorns, presence of lions.

I. Title.
PS3563.0889A57   811'.5'4   75-30765
ISBN 0-316-58580-7
ISBN 0-316-58581-5 pbk.

Published simultaneously in Canada
by Little, Brown & Company (Canada) Limited

PRINTED IN THE UNITED STATES OF AMERICA

For John, Catherine, Megan,
Maeve, Catherine, and Ciannat Howett

Acknowledgments

Some of these poems first appeared in the following publications: "Sir John by Starlight" in *The Kenyon Review*; "Pastoral," "The Danaides," "Circe and her lovers," "The Dice," and "Light-Year" in *Poetry*; "Kennesaw Mountain" in *The Southern Review*; "Our Third President" in *Southern Voices*; an early version of "Shiloh" in *The Dekalb Literary Arts Journal*; "Peggy Lee Douglas at the Dulcimer" and "Sentry" in *Cold Mountain Review*; "Above Dalton" in *Southern Poetry Review*; "Sourwood Mountain Song" in *The Mississippi Review*; "Mirabelle" in *The Georgia Review*.

Grateful acknowledgement is made to these magazines for permission to reprint the poems, and also to these publishers: The Richmond Intercultural Center for the Humanities, 1 West Main Street, Richmond, Virginia, for the later version of "Shiloh," which appeared in their publication "A Borrower Be"; and The Borestone Mountain Poetry Awards Anthologies, Solana Beach, California, for "Sir John By Starlight," which appeared in "Best Poems of 1964".

I am also grateful to Emory University for the time to finish "T H E L E T T E R S".

Unfortunately, the poem "Cold Harbor," which belongs to the group "The Unpeaceable Kingdom," Part II, could not be included here as the breaking of the long lines would have changed the poem. It appears in the Summer of 1974 number of *The New Orleans Review*.

Contents

Book One

THE LETTERS

"G-d drew them [THE LETTERS],
hewed them, combined them,
weighed them, and through them
produced the whole creation
and everything that is destined
to be created."

The Sefer Yetshirah, or Book of Creation

The Letters I

How A came first when THE LETTERS waited

Some were too forward. They were put back
Some made up the syllables of Death
They came after

Some made up together the name of Justice
They were hidden in the middle

"If it is the world you seek there can be no justice
and if it is justice you seek there can be no world"

These letters were mingled
that the world might be made

How great A came before all and how it was spoken
Aleph and Alpha
of the two tribes
of the oxen and the axes

How it held up the world in a hundred aspects
How one of these
was the Titan Atlas

And how Chaos cried out against A
It was the first taking

How the teacher spoke sternly the letter A to the children
and how the sages smiled at his emphasis

Without A, where were we?
In the erasing of the scroll
we were the fine shavings of sheepskin
Mercy and Love were not
Death, first, there might be, or Justice

Myths I

In the beginning

we are assured there was a garden
palisaded   PARADISE
                 (from the Persian)
with a white horsehair
of water
ascending
          in the heat

AZIMUTH and ZERO
                 (from the Arabic)
on the hottest days

as in Italian gardens still
                 white marble
                 dark trees

against the glare
there was water
                 Primal matter
and the sound of water
and the echo of water
                 the tumbling of doves
                 and their converse
                 in accord

————Where did the water come from?

————It was the let of stones
                 and it is present
                 smaller
                 more lively
                 than the eye of a pigeon
                 in the hardest flint

4

————How came the water before the stone?

————It was there before the stone
and the stones came to guard it
but stones also were of water once
was not paradise palisaded?

There was petrification even in paradise
It enclosed the zero

Myths II

"And such was the intensity of the heat that many were
turned into glass, together with the finer matter about them"

> Question: Was this fable or fact?
> STORY or HISTORY having the same root in Greek
> "A TRUE HISTORY" or "A TRUE STORY"—see
> translations of Lucian

Yet imagine it—
turned into glass

of what color?

Assume the predominate color was blue
the color of darkness visible
the second light of the candle of Cabbalah
and also the robes of the bards were blue
worshippers of Andraste, goddess of the Druids

Let us take blue for the ground
and a cast of purple

blue bottle glass of the sea
and of the Virgin of Guadalupe
in Mexico

people of blue glass
outlasting those of grass
of dust
of A-dam
red clay

but co-equal in eternity
with those of volcanic dust
at Pompeii

and at Hiroshima
there were only shadows

If I am to speak of
metamorphosis
or metempsychosis

—and the dolls of Dresden

"Horrible to think of it"
                    Virgil

and more horrible
surely
to accept a part in it

Those living in an era of
such metamorphosis
should not throw anything

"Metamorphoseos wot what I mene"
says Chaucer's Man of Law

and where is the law now?
only mutability

Alchemical change of men

The true lights of G-d
in Gnosis
Marcion for one

scattered, fragmented

children of blue glass
saints in crystal

Let us assume anything

In history is all story
and the splinters
of manglass

Myths III

What stirred the dust?—

What stirred the dust?
the worm

as the wind stirred
the laurel leaves

The earthworms remake the Earth
many times over
in each generation

it is not man
but the worm
that remakes Earth

who shall discover
such greatness?

It is sealed in silence
and a man studies himself

Myths IV

Was there a Woman before Eve?

Before Eve there was the
idea of women
and it touched the Earth

It was not Lilith
but a rumor
nameless

A woman goes into her house
Eve is here
and the hours of Eve

but the nameless is still
unnamed

and the Earth
expectant

Adam Names the Animals

Ac
Bez
Cuf
Di
Eop
Faw
Ginzal
Hut
Ipoth
Ji
Koz
Letlak
Mutal
Nepsa
O
Petzut
Quegor Upta
Rabu
Samsa
Tuton Obi
Ul
Vetzma
Wyst
Xtor Aa
Yu
Zept

Myths V

How shall we tell eternity in a ring?
and Alexander stood here
and Hitler there?

And if it be the rings of a tree
the tree is upon the ring
and the blade of the axe in the earth

and if it be the rings in water
shall they outlast
the sound of the falling stone?

The sound of the stone
will outlast its fall
going into another stone
which is within the ring

and if no man can hear it
what then?

We are near the beginning of things
and the sounds of the Battle of Actium
are in the waves still

Myths VI

How animals may be lured by a sweet smell
is a pretty trick
and the matter of many theses

but though everyone knows how a unicorn may
be taken
there is no captive unicorn
to prove the success of the experiment

not—let us be charitable—
for lack of virgins, or mirrors, or combs
only for lack of unicorns

Yet who is to say
that the absence of unicorns
has not been a greater thing
than the presence of lions?

It is the sweet smell of the unicorn
that has lured men

How tactful this test of
virginity
not of maidens only
but of the most refined scholars

This is a long tower of ivory
that shines
in the moonlight

And a man may lack
musk, or civet, or rosewater

and grow mad of love
on an absence of unicorns

Myths VII

"Some of the diseased hold themselves like dead
and others believe they are of glass"

—so Conrad of Magenberg on diseases of the spleen

And there have been young girls also
in the time of adolescence
who believed they were turning
by hours before the glass into glass
undone by ambition
and by their imagination also

Others thought themselves lifted aloft
by rocs from remote mountain valleys of Arabia

set in portions of meat
thrown down
by the devious hunters

and were recovered
Shamirs
or diamonds

unbreakable lights
though lidded
until the cutters
of polyhedra
in polyhedra
created them eyes

so they became in themselves
moving starmaps

12

infinite changing
manifestations
of fire
on the dark foilcloth
of nights

But the more brittle sick
feared everything

the least jar or
collision
of the bed they lay in
or the hands of the nurse

being not diamonds
but common glass

that the kiss of a loved one
might shatter

a fallen spoon
or even
the accident
of their own breathing

These reflected nothing
from a mass of bedclothes

only the fear of touch
a glazing of terror

Myths VIII

"Peace to the beaver," says the writer of
The Flowers of Virtue

And indeed this creature has much honor
in all bestiaries
who being hunted for his testicles
which were needed in medicine
emasculated himself
and so went free
and the hunters in health
and in profit
drank to the beaver

Honor the beaver
but what is this virtue?

Beast and man
should die as they were made
even a priest
—though not one of Cybele's

Peace at too high price

Beast and man—
we should be tempted as we were made
It is our honor to wear the days
and nights out in turmoil
—excepting the Stoics

Of love and lust there is plainly no cure
but time or the teeth of the beaver

The Letters II

————What were THE LETTERS doing?

They were behind the letters
the little letters before the great

in Xhosa
in Zuni
in Kymric
in cant
in gabble

In the play of the ballad
also in the sermon

They crowded the line
like swallows
no tail angled the same
They were alone like a fly
shining on a gatepost

They were an anthill disturbed
They were hornets erupting forth

They were tsi tsi
They were Moog Moog

They were bath-kol
They were Maa-mar

In microphones they were magnified
They whispered softly
in autophones
through the windpipes of cranes

On the seabed and in the hurricane
they crackled
they crowed and spoke

They stalked the hills
They slept in sealed chambers
They danced in the rings

They were as sibilant
as a snake in dry leaves
They fractured like a fall of tiles

They were Arum Arum
They were nu'voo nu'voo

They hung on both sides of the head
like beards
like twin swarms of bees

They buried their dead
They escaped in excelsior

They were erased
They clapped hands in the flames

They were unraveled by moths
The silverfish licked them with its tail

They bred like a banquet of worms
They lay in levels like ten Troys

They ran fast together
they were a starling pack
they were a press of minnows
they were tadpoles
they were live writing
on the bed of streams

They were set together
in a bed of lead

They were dished from the printer's tray
They were scrambled by devils

They assumed importance
They undid their doing
They honored an oath
They broke their word

They were erased
They formed fours and conquered

They were all and nothing
they were only the letters
before THE LETTERS

Largest and least
they made up the telling of men

Myths IX

How one of the sages heard a bird singing
inside the tomb of a king
is a riddle not easy to be answered

for the tomb was of stone and in
eloquent footnotes he assures us
there was no crack in the sides
and the slab was in place

We cannot conjecture a cricket
out of the text
for the plain sense of the word
is bird
Nor would a hidden spring
account for the sound
nor some trick of the wind

How a bird could live enclosed in a tomb
and why it should sing there
we have no answer for

Yet the sage was not old
nor at fault upon other occasions

In discourse on the spleen of the wren
or in the method of resting by seabirds
he follows the correct models

In authority and observation
he is hardly to be bettered
while his follower
Anthony
tells of his master's delight
in the drumming of quails

One so scrupulous elsewhere
cannot be held to account
for an error of fact

yet the strangeness remains

Myths X

In the month of Athyr
when the leaves sleep
after their restlessness
when the rains
press on one another
like lovers
when the waters are mingled
the greater waters
and the least
when the eaves
and the gutters
are full of singing
when the black rat
slides by the river
when the stubble
is furred
when men walk
with their heads down
when they carry their clothes
like houses
like little homesteads of safety
like snails

Adam Names the Precious Stones

Afa
Bak
Cof Abor As
Dja
Eis
Fazma
Gamrak
Hiop
Illor
Ja Asp Ja
Kissac
Lut
Mar Jid Esp
Noio Nag Noio
Ovvbakram
Pazur
Quijo Iod
Rubuzril
Sammansar
Totfeyrak
Ul
Vagasvag Shem
Waa Kepsur
Xuxus
Yitjuf
Zimats

Myths XI

And the tree by the water

Excepting all who passed
and did not stop to see

how many yellow blossoms in its boughs
how many glistening branches in the winter
how many birds

——nothing was always there

And the tree by the water

Excepting all who passed
and stopped but did not see

how its bark ran with rain
how close it came to trailing in the water
those furthest leaves
how water rose at times to meet it

————nothing was always there

And the tree by the water

Excepting all who saw
but did not see

And the tree by the water
The tree by the water

It was not Zion we lamented
It was our exile
from our very lives

Myths XII

"What is glass but still water?"

——so Jarry

Very still

It is the breaking of surfaces
that excites expectation
as in bathing in a still sea
there is recognition
that eras
are about to pass out of the blood

unrealized realization
there is division yet
no simple matter of skin

And in Venice
where glass is made
near a quiet sea
the palaces
blown from the feet of palaces
are almost perfect

where there is a flaw
it is a mere bubble

Easy to extend ourselves
at least by appearances
to sense the blood growing cooler
to enter
by the marine second door of palaces

Where is the flaw?

What is a bubble but air?

What do the glass blowers
blow around us?

What is it goes with us always
when we pass through surfaces
with our surfaces?

Myths XIII

And both ascend
two themes together
separate
and intertwined

the voices
of Tristan
and Isolde

or hawks
soaring
clockwise
and anti-
clockwise
over the valley
of the Harle

their marriage rings
made in the air

one circle
on another

or Chambord stair

three examples
in which the one
is sprung out of the earth
upon the counter moving
spiral
of the other

and each sustained there
in the perilous air

only in revolutions
of the opposite

Myths XIV

As Lucian: "Amber and the swans
have made me eloquent
upon all subjects"

As to the doorman answered Lugh:
"A poet I, I come from Appled Eamhain
of swans and yewtrees"

Under the bow of a bridge
in apple breathing autumn
yew trees for foil
bright beads of amber
about their bodies sail
white and repeating white
the swans
of words, of eloquence

Myths XV

How apples were so often passwords
how they were magic to Merlin and many others
how the Field of Apple Trees was the Place of Presence
                    in the *Zohar*
and how the king came to Avalon, the Isle of Apple Groves
to be restored after the grievous hurt at Camlann

How angels thirsted for the fruit of apples
and how the applespray makes marriages in heaven
and how the Rood was made of applewood
how Adam's seed was with the seed of apples
in secret store so many dark years in the cave

How the seed hangs in chambers like a lamp
how the spur shoots of apple trees bear flowers
how apple blossom frenzies men as well as moths
and yet how apples are the antidote for love

All these are mysteries beyond the text
Wisdom in apples who shall pare away?

The Letters III

——— What were THE LETTERS doing?

In Lucian, in Rimbaud's *Voyelles*
they paraded, they showed
their ways

in the *Correspondances* of Baudelaire
gracefully
gratefully
they accepted echoes

In the translations
of translations
in the hear-say
of hearsay

their shapes were shadows
they were weighed like weights
they lost their salt, their savor
they were like stoppered vials
they were like glassy bones
they were like white statues

In the rings
they were revenants

In the uniformity of type
they were the ghosts of voices

In the plainness of their end
they were the little letters
they diminished to a dot

Myths XVI

They were talking about stones
about the properties and holiness of stones

of Gervais of Tilbury and many others
Hebrews and Arabs
who had studied stones

In the afternoon
when the motes climbed in the sunlight
they were talking together about stones

about the turquoise sensitive to men's ills
about the amethyst that cures drunkenness
about the alsarik that heals eyes

In the afternoon
when the throat of the ostrich melts the gold
they were talking together about stones

Myths XVII

"I began to learn a new alphabet and meditate on words that
            hissed and words that gasped"

——so said Jerome, and there are many alphabets

How many alphabets?—of the oxen and the axes?

What syllables the thunder spoke and the water
and the hammer among the rocks
the camel and the jackal
what Attis said to Attis among the pinetrees
and the voice breathing in the cedars
after Babel

Many alphabets and many tongues
yet each tongue matched to a little piece of earth
Adam, Adamah, Adam Kadmon—
of the red clay
or of the white
of crystallite, of ochre, of cinnabar
in the geology and geography of tongues after alphabets
and before alphabets

Define it downward
Is it not the pietas of a few fields
an unknown allegiance
as the water of a certain well is known
and the wine of a particular acre?

"O Taste and See"—
Is it not the abracadabra of the roots
and what nourishes the roots—
as the farmer first crumbles the loam
and after, the grainhead in his hands?

Is it not also the overcast of exile
the many accents of exile?
And who is not learnéd in leaving?

Lingua franca and Shibboleth of the earth
of the race and of every removal

Adam Names the Stars

Azlahim
Besuur
Chafchas
Dunihhaboz
Es Os Es
Fetf
Gemaznut Babil
Hasmasos
Iffafalur
Jomachai
Kimah Hamar
Lyahorabin
Muxust Isus Ior
Neyomar Abar
Ottixoxos
Pezragil
Quem Raffeen
Rymihoassam
So Amahal
Tukoorak Assur
Unffa Esparosin
Vobbehar
Wessesibbi
Xhorizames
Yesutza
Zibossamoxibistar

Myths XVIII

Wise was the sage
who told the man maddened with fear
by his own shadow
to study light

Yet no Dives, nor even
a poorer citizen
who had breakfasted
would know

how the first color
seen upon a day
after long fasting
may mend the spirit
for a while
or grow so terrible
inside the head

no study of the light
could put it right

Myths XIX

How Ulysses answered to No-name
and how Tristan
feigning madness
answered King Mark
"My father was an old hack
and my mother a ewe"

How No-name prospered
and how the disguised Tristan
butted the king's ewe

How Nemo invisible
walks in and steals
wine from the cup
cake from the platter
and then goes off to Nowhere
when the found thieves hang
under the trees
like seedpods

How the Have-names held a conference
and how Absent was chosen
How the Unknown Knight
taunted Sir Dinadan
How Anonymous went first
in the Anthology
and how It ravaged a country
and blew dust at the challenger

How All-in-All
outsmarted Solomon
and how she-she and he-he
bedded down in the marketplace

How Know-Nothing blamed Nobody
How the scholars argued over "ex Nihilo"
How the schools were divided, "Nemo" and "Nullus"
How mere nothing became Sir Somebody
and how often he regretted it
How the goddess responded to no one
and was worshipped by everyone

How the trees were name tagged by the Botanist
and how they remained rooted
How there was no river called Danube or Rhine
How the sea resisted Canute
And how love languished for the naming

——How all love went out in the wake of the name
like the riddle in unriddling

Adam Names the Flowers and Trees

Ap Uris
Balaffa
Cyomunda
Daxeyiis
Eiopia
Fii
Geomar
Hybor Eznabor
Ipylis
Jayomynthos
Kastrabel
Lynthelysum
Mar
Nixypys
Op Ramp Aiy
Pastrapel
Querror
Razwaxtzelen
Spasippi
Tor
Ubrellmar
Vad As Falla
Wo
Xasffyon
Yexta Aklagor
Zytheris

Myths XX

Consider the Aleut Indians
their alphabet of hunger

In a little while
a is in absence
b in the beaks of seabirds
c in cutwater and crags
d in dreams of the feast

How close the hills come
How sharp are stones

After so many days
the stomach turns on itself
the gnawing of the wolf
the whittling of whalebone
the strain of a windlass

Then a membrane is pinched
nail comes in under nail
awl punches sailcloth
and the spirit speaks
as iron balks
at a knot in hardwood

How soon thereafter
all this is forgotten
The huge appetite of pain
abated, goes elsewhere

nothing is near
no moss now fragrant

What is left of the head
praises privation
without words worships
the grown god Hunger

Myths XXI

"Souls do not sleep like dormice"

——so Raleigh

Indeed, but no soft thing at rest
without a shell

——Tread on the eggshells, angels

No pin
without unnumbered seraphim

What is secret of secret
will not anatomize

Disturb even a seed sleeping
and you harvest stones

For the old emblematist
the World Fire sleeps in a flint

Not Prometheus his fennel
carries a greater threat—

not an atom without—

That was some Great World
hidden, yet
anatomized!

But who shall probe the atom of atoms
out of its shell?

Who shall awake the soul sleeping its sleep?

Not Descartes find it in a gland
nor Boyle
in a drop of dew

Each generation renumbers the stars
Given as many generations
shall they reach the sum?

No pin
without unnumbered seraphim

——Tread on the eggshells, angels

Infinite secret mansions
where the soul coils in

Myths XXII

Even as the light going declares the darkness
So there was no sure knowing
Not anywhere sharp as a shadow
Absence assured the outline only

Even as sickness discovered every part
Not for a map the terra incognita
Displace of space
Near weight of unseen bodies

What ghosts believe in ghosts believe in—
Only without you there, said Strindberg
Was even madness real enough to bear

Myths XXIII

The tale tells how the letter T was in touch
and in Tristan falling from the tower
and how the lepers clutched at Isolde

What song sang Tristan in the air
seeing the sea so far below
and the surf like a scarf
how many times it came back on the sea's arm
and how the birds flew forward and back
beneath Tristan

when he saw the sun shine on the rocks
like the yellow points of the broom
when he touched the air
and not Isolde?

What were the sea mews calling in his ear
as he fell so far
so many minutes in the air?

He anticipated the sea
He felt cold come into his bones

He touched the foreland and the bay
With five fingers he caressed all Cornwall
With five he stroked the Forest of Morois
and with five the forest of the sea

He lay over the iron shadow
of Lethowstow, lost Lyonesse
as he had lain over Isolde

The tale tells how he escaped
that he sat naked on a rock in the middle of the sea
and he laughed outright:

"How to tell you, Cymry, of a lover's leap
How to tell you!"

And what song sang Isolde among the lepers
their skin against her skin
the plump of her white arm
in the hooks of their fingers?

How they clutched at the Queen
not fire so urgent
not the embrace of Tristan

and her marrow ached
under the skin, within the bone

"Is there another love, my love
the love of the hawthorn for the snow
the love of a stake for the winter sea
the love of the Man in the Moon?

"Is there another love, my love
the loved flesh for the fallen
the body beloved in a pelt of pain?

"And after this company
will you find me whole?
Will even I know my Eve's skin
from the thorn and the foliage?

"Will I leave our bed for the Moon
for the wolf-tones of briar?"

Truth ruthless in touch
So for a season is broken
the old spell
the enduring thing
like a sword
like a word misspoken
by air, by a lazar's hand
parted the lovers
the most faithful of lovers

ABACAZA

abacadaeafagahaiajakalamanaoapaqarasatauavawaxayaz

	color		match	
sound match	a	as	in	smell match
	b	as	in	
	c	as	in	
	d	as	in	
	e	as	in	
	f	as	in	
	g	as	in	
	h	as	in	
	i	as	in	
	j	as	in	
	k	as	in	
	l	as	in	
	m	as	in	
	n	as	in	
	o	as	in	
	p	as	in	
	q	as	in	
	r	as	in	
	s	as	in	
	t	as	in	
	u	as	in	
	v	as	in	
	w	as	in	
	x	as	in	
	y	as	in	
taste match	z	as	in	touch match

Myths XXIV

What was the song of Arthur in his sadness?

"Bitter the frost, bitter the tree, bitter the stone
bitter the white wave of the sea
that in this island
men should be born so mean"

Roebuck, badger, and raven
What song sang Bran's head
as it swung in the wind?

"Bitter the bread, bitter the wine, bitter the company
of those who come after

"If the windows on old grief are open
what comfort is kept
in the little house of winter
in barton, hanger, and coombe?"

Dogfox, lapwing, and salmon
What song sang Merlin in the maiden's rock?

"Better the silence, better the wind in the thorns
What treasure if letters lie loreless?
What craftspell endures in the earth?

"What profit the old leaves lost
to a plot green as parsley
old tales of serpents and moons
or the Babel of waves far off?"

Myths XXV

All the Proud Walkers

Were they stars
or pilgrims?

"Here and Everywhere"
their motto

with staff
and scallop shell

like the samara
winged seed of the elm
blown by the world's wind
across the world

Time is the outward aspect
of Eternity

"The little owl
upon the eaves
watches the sun go down"
—so Virgil

One sun, one journey
here and everywhere

Myths XXVI

How they came to Killiwic
the old and the young
under the circles
of the buzzard hawks

40

Green wheat marked out the ramparts
the fosse was of dark briar

The flint with its sealed flame
blocked the ear of the warrior

A child could count the spirals on its fingers:

> ONE as in those very fingers
> TWO as in the coiled beast sleeping
> THREE as in the gold ring of the sea princess of Tyre
> FOUR as in the castle of Arianrhod
> FIVE as in the cross section of a young apple tree

and there were many more

How many more?

As many as the puzzle in a children's book—
counting the faces in the foliage

Who picks up the thread of the maze
never walks straight

Who takes up the riddle of the dance
dances in eight

Who comes by different levels in the latter day
is never late

neither a second Dylan by the track of green
nor any other Merlin by the briar

But What Is

"But what is Paradise? All things that are . . . save
one tree and the fruits thereof . . ."

By the dark glass and the clear
what shall be prophesied of Paradise?

One shadow overall
of the tree
                like a mighty river
Fruit in the skin of fruit
forever remembered   as once
under the rind   and always

                        all seasons and everywhere
                        shared

The Letters IV

——What were THE LETTERS doing?

They were laughing among themselves

——Were they like actors in the wings?

No, they were like children
even the terrible ones

They had no mind to men
They were not even laughing at men

They were mocking each other—
their colors and shapes
their scents and sounds

They were miming and mimicking
the taste of S
the texture of L

They were somersaulting and dancing
They were trying on disguises
They were waiting for new worlds

Book Two

THE UNPEACEABLE KINGDOM

Unfinished America

unfinished america the raw orange pelt of the beaver and the road
ving out in the clay between ghost gray cotton bushes somewhere
south georgia and the mountains the axel and heart breaking rock

ights where abraham somebody sacrificed isaac his last this third
ay of september eithteen-fifty-one to the god of endurance and had
o strength left to bury his son but gave him to the birds of the air

ad the apple brown woman born county clare by the door of her sod house in
omewhere nebraska maybe giving a look to the land all around her that would
ay a man down to an animal scream knowing his debts had all come home and no

ed left to plant for the next season or even in the calvinist cold
urial lots of new england unsettled settled the restless anger with
od and with england and the huckster and preacher rasping and whittling

ie conscience barebone frenzied with unfinished business and even henry
avid thoreau's enterprise lock stock and barrel declared bankrupt on two
ents a day and his beanrows going back to the wilderness and only the lilac

vely luxurious sweet scented seeming to mock at the stonepicker stone
reaker stone carver stone farmer paying his way in the panic of this year
r that and the fish bones shoring up credit and the lifers making a new

ontract to be quit of their god-debts by fall at the latest and move on
ove anywhere to the beautiful barrens the mocking bird singing and the
ophers loafing and the passenger pigeons darkening the sky by day and

unfinished america . . .

Peggy Lee Douglas at the Dulcimer

What cavalier at Nasby dead
Had a coat turned
By a farmer's daughter?
What brine has dyed
The while silk green
As it floated over the water?

So fond a favor and so flawed
With a heart of cross stitch
Half unlucky
And a doeskin band
Tacked round the edge
As it came to west Kentucky.

No sulphur rose
In the dark brake grows
So fair as your hair, Mat Allen;
And no dress could wrest
The cold from my breast
When the owls call down the valley.

Our Third President

In the gardens of Monticello
            little mountain?
            sweet little mountain?
there is a sign
        EXIT AND TOMB
and in Charlottesville
on the campus of the University of Virginia
a serpentine wall one brick thick
invention of Thomas Jefferson
third president and Cincinnatus
of the young republic

who under giant trees
and in an impressively ugly stone monument
sleeps
where brown tree frogs and green garden snakes
jump or skitter among the
large leaves
turned dark side up
and black bog earth
full of white threads

In all his inventions
a man must be faithful
to himself

"There is genius
even in his failures"
says one character of
another in
Thomas Love Peacock's novel *Gryll Grange*

There is a style in bringing forth a desk
or a clock or an unconventional house

also in writing a declaration or
designing a serpentine wall
that thinly meanders
only as intended

or in building a monument
which was not his invention

or in ordering a sign
which he did not intend
to be part of his garden

North West Passaging

I see the crossing of light on two stalks
the bone china clicks together in the cupboard
the old woman draws closer to the fire the
palest of flames Montana and the morning
and a horse running off something stronger
than the gad of a fly in a far meadow some
wildness other than the youth and the beast
fever in its blood a madness of being maybe a
thing to fear watching and watching for the
slow movement of red clouds and the shadows
of peaks here the river brought us and now
pushes us out into eddy water into the slack of
motion an eerie suspension of the former
drive and the rocker rocks and rocks the
china in the cupboard at the edge of things
like a ripple running out but unlike the
hoofbeat of the young horse with the frenzy
of itself running through the roots of the grass
to the steps and the boards under my feet

To have come so far driven by the force of
I say the river something like a river
a river in flood carrying all this and
the two of us to shore everything under the
impassable peaks in this place of meadows
where what carried us suddenly slackened or
nudged us like an animate thing to the side of
the uprights of a bridge the bone china and
the cupboard the rocker and a mess of dresses

And the horse still running and the rocker
still rocking and the sun hardening on the
grass and the clouds still passing changing
their colors very slowly the beat of the
hooves driven out of my legs resisting

the undertoe easily the faint pull back
into the frenzied gait of the colt and
the old woman trying to make heat from
the flames and the flames paler
frailer than sunlight to have come so
far only to watch and rock and have missed
whatever it was without even sensing
the moment it happened and knowing
only the miss of it now and the beat
going down into roots of the grass
and the mountains reversed and the
river and light and the heat
outside us and passing
between them

Far Floridas

Night moving and the fixed full moon
over the swamplands where birds' voices start
the rumor of great journeys

Frogs are the shipwrights of the shipwrecked earth
Methuselahs before De Leon came
old bearded man
looking for moving water

Live logs propel themselves
in the Ur-Eden
vast ripples black and white

The cypress stains and stains

A quiet of clouds

No going from here
What the intruder seeks
beyond far Floridas

No flower uncabled
Bearded with weed
the fleet is anchored here

Put out the flares
Ambiguous sirens never lied
They too were old

Whatever fountain sought   he finds
His youth unguessed at   Night and paradise

II

Chickamauga   *For Bell Wiley*

white lightning on black water of the swamp magnesium flares
pitch on their bodies and the giddy licks as fire
comes up the creeks catching at bushes crumpled heaps
of clothes that rise up rigid then slump back
into the ashes as the fire pours on
over the water over the lines of men

give me a rope of vine to grope at give me more water
give me a way to reach you through my pain

across the tranquil acid slopped in Brady's tray out of
the sepia prints hung up like skins to dry

to scream in the mosquitoes' wail or burn aglow
in fireflies crossing now the wastes you know
cool lids of twilight Chickamauga's risen trees

Kennesaw Mountain

At Kennesaw we piece together from pine needles
and undulating earth, old trenches, old positions,
guarding a clearing. Sunlight on the boughs
of chestnut, oak, blue pine, once walls of foam
that let the Israelites across, then closed

on the Egyptians. Did the Promised Ones
stay one day longer? Here was the Killing Ground
for clear-eyed farmers' boys. Tumult and forming blue,
misted by rain-soaked grass and wraiths of smoke,
still better targets than racoons or the quick squirrels
that never pressed to die in living lines
dressed by the right. A saber catching light. A brilliant rag
bobbing and dancing from the smoke on some gay errand,
twitched on by wires. It draws the firing up
into the sunlight. Hangs there for counted seconds. Falls.
And you are cheering out of dry mouths. Nothing looks changed,
but you are winning. The blue files stay, but these are dead.
The smoke is thinning. Birdsong returns. As now,
the woods seem still.

              You'd won. You held the line,
older, half starved, exhausted, but unbroken—
until the horseman comes to Kennesaw
to say you've been outflanked once more, that Sherman
swings South—ignores you—South, into your homeland.
And you must fill in what you held with dead and follow
to pick up what he leaves.

              We find your victory
more bitter than defeat, who keep our eyes alert,
watch other clearings; coughing through nights of rain,
Stand To for other mornings. We called you to a truce
this afternoon to succor what survived before your earthworks,
but no one came. It's six o'clock, the Forest Ranger
waits patient in his truck. He'll close these acres
after our settled dust with a long chain of links . . .
Oh tell us what you saw. Nothing is won or lost
at Cheatham Hill, Kolb Farm, and Kennesaw.

Shiloh

The lot of the fathers all remember the rain and the broken chapel
at Shiloh tabernacle of the ancients and the yellow wounds of
so many pines there were more men felled than trees but it was
the trees that bled yellow in Miller's mind for ten years after
the event now Miller is trying to unbuckle his belt to let the
swelling inside make a Punchinello out of him four men face him
sitting as though round a campfire and each one has the same
exactly the same bullet wound in the forehead almost without
blood it is papers not blood they have turned out their pockets
of playing cards letters string old newspapers desecration of groves
when the kings came to Shiloh when Esau saw the gray pottage of the
young men scattered he wept the inheritance was Jacob's he slept in
Bethel seeing the angels climb a ladder of wounded trees he was
mortified with the remembrance of what his landgain had led to he was
exiled in his own heart and the land that was his now was nothing
was an abomination he was rich in the hatred of dead men the ark
was lifted out of the mud and sand and carried to Pittsburg Landing
where Grant the dark lion sucked at a dead cigar and moaned like
Paul in madness I brought you back into Egypt Cairo and Memphis
to fester away the pines are as yellow as Custer's hair they are
running resin like rivers of honey they are the lights of groves
they lead men into union a united states of the night the
surgeons' lanterns are beautiful in the tents as sulphur
butterflies the limbs of Rameses are laid at their door
they struggle in mud but are separate who has sunk under here
who has lost the meadow out of his eyes as the wagons unburden
: the patient horses black mud to their eyes are bearing away
the ground stampers the builders of cities it is a Beelzebub
of flies we have established here east of Eden the chaplains
and looters are abroad in the land they spy out gold mice
among garments rolled in blood one touches Miller who pretends to

be dead as hands take out a Bible from under his shirt remove the
ten dollar bill let the Bible drop into his lap crawl away to
the paper searching through it taking nothing there is nothing
to take may the ten dollars stolen turn him to salt may shame
make a beast of him howling repentance at stones this is the
pay of the day species got with the milling of men it is not good
in the eyes of God it is no longer a marker in His book He bears not
with conceits of the braggard He will deal in the dark with the
wrongdoer it is well away what was earned for this harvest His pages
stain with my blood did I not know His signs that I sinned
was I an innocent that I went with the daughters of Lilith
and made with the strangers of cities this second covenant to be a
worker of wrath do Thou God with me as Thou willest he is eased up
cursing against further trespass carried off on a cart to the Landing
how did I come to this place he asks an old man with a knife
was I better than they who lie out in the rain was I chosen

Above Dalton

where we were standing when the rain walked round us
with a jingle of mule tackle on the piney air
and a cat snicker of hog flesh twisting on a stick
like a live snake trying to get itself up
backing out of the fire
and a jug of buttermilk

brought by some girl so lean and piney herself
in her wet shreds of floursacks my heart hit me
not for love but the poor peakish look of her
and for bringing up buttermilk

coming up that mountain in the snarl of a spring morning
to a camp of men who were no better than you'd guess us
and setting the jug down on a stone like we'd ordered it
and going off without a smile or a word down the path she'd come up

above Dalton one day in the war when the rain walked round us

Gaines Mill

read into this my reading I was the shade page of
Hector that hour in a gloom of trees and have
intervening
surrendered nothing not the sting of an
insect nor the odor of the guns

though Achilles cried out from the trench yet the
bells of Troy were nearer behind me it was the
last light of the day I was sixteen that summer alone
and how many were with me

there were apples there. Now some say there were no
apples in the pit of the valley but I say I saw
apples and smelt them and the mash of them under
men's feet in the hurrying

and I was amazed equally by blood and the way
the ground sucked up the essence of men it was
greedily it was hog like and black lipped
and I was afraid to be drained
from the soles of my boots
in the shallows

and I thought of you in the time of the splintering of trees
and my bones aching not to be snapped I remembered you

drawing your skirts up a little to be out of the dust
as you walked down the road away from me
going home I suppose in the cool of the dusk
I remembered you

not that your name was Helen who had laughed at the book
and the fancy of it
nor would you see me nor know that your name was my armor

not for the shaming of you Andromache nor for causes
except that that city should stand for my Troy
I was shamelessly neutral

but say your name now is it lost let it linger a little
and I buoyant in blood and unkillable
crash through the mass of the Greeks
oh the terrible Myrmidons

hack for the ridge in my rage in the tumult the crackling
of underbrush buffet of bodies the hewing
breaking like fence posts before me
the waste of their faces
press through their lives
the hot charge of their breath
and the chime of their buttons

but for you I survived on that night is it easy
to see near that house on the brow of the hill we had taken
in my jacket of blood I am photographed still
by the glare of the Argives' bright boats

it's for you I am smiling

Sourwood Mountain Song

like a saw snagged in wood
ten years and every word she said
the whine and the clasp of grain

a line of Byron and an old song
about Miss Mousie and the courting frog
and the war came and I was roving
and the teeth stopped in the log

then the silence was like a knot
even when bullets snapped trees
I was listening always listening
and the killing went on over my head
like the tune of a liquored up fiddler
and the boards bucked under the dancers' feet

and I went roving in the moon
the woodsman's moon and the soldier's
and ached for the listening and thought
of the bullfrog courting and Miss Mousie
and the small white teeth of the saw

and nothing of this I shook off
till I came to Sourwood Mountain in the Spring
and hung up my gun and drank cold creek water
and saw the leaf claws on a rock like a bear's
and the gold sand in the bottom of the stream

and made up a song to go with the circle
I'd walked any weather and under the moon
how the fiddler'd be sawing there still
and how sourwood made the sweetest honey

Sentry

when the squirrels tobogganed down the tiles in
darkness over our heads and the wind knocked out
its pipe against the panes like father on the
hob of the fire and the boards of the old house
about us stretched until I thought the nails
would be popped out of their holes like bullets

brother we shivered under the quilt our insides
sloppy and aching we counted off a third breathing
thing in the room and made massacres of the fire
tiptoeing under us where our scalped parents slept

later years we each slipped over windowsills to be off
in the night in the same or in different directions
crossing borders in darkness at the same call of wars

and now my brass buttons taint with their ominous
smell the chill air before dawn and click like a
catch drawn or a fingered bullet when I brush on
the split rail I stand at to watch in the woods
the eight shades of black exchange edges

what animal walkers or birds stalk over my
shrilling skin and what dry leaf scrapes
its razor block and wanders metallic under
my chin what rat mixes its hair with my hair

while you visit me either alive or dead for the
letter's late which army you never said yet
you near me and what fearful whispered tale
do we dare tell across dark against fear

pass kinsman
by blood only neither by left side nor right

Malvern Hill   *For Jean Farley*

late summer sun drawing the swastikas or sundisks of the wheels
in shadow wide across the wheat from guns
and the crows' clamor swallows skimming stalks
of guinea gold
on the plateau the river's loop a scimitar of steel
or section of another greater gun wheel
and in each quarter massed quieter than clumps of men
the quiet trees

below the slope debris of broken charges blows the poppy red
blue ribband band white stars of banners and in a corner
of a split rail fence holding against his chest the staff of
one such battle flag sits Clayton as if thrown
into that angle by main force

black powder tobacco oozings flies
ferment about his mouth his hat like a squashed piecrust
under one hand still flopping fluttering
as frantic as a bird
some pinioned fledgling
involuntary quick
tries to escape the nerve's dead center
in the man

Listen to me you angels
perusing avenues
strands of white sand and oyster shells
under live oaks and moss

Listen to me you angels island ghosts
the white robed spooks of slaves

61

Listen to me you angels come at last
over scrubbed Sunday benches over piers
where the white bobbing rowboats ride
blue Carolina bays

Listen to me you white birds of the swamp
or the brown pelican flotillas
of the sea

Come to me now come gather up the bread
in broken picnic bits spectres of peace
long promised peace
come with your baskets
dressed for the markets on the mainland
come

Mirabelle

what the avenue led to
only a child's rocking horse rocking
on the lawn and two diamond studs
at my feet just the right
distance between them
to be a man's eyes
or a woman's
shining up
each with a glimmer of orange
out of brown laurel leaves
and a patch
of odorous black mud

the noon hour
so oppressive in sunlight
it set the faces of stopped clocks
everywhere
in tree limbs
and the same cracked pattern
timed tributaries
split second stations
of spiderwork
in walls

only the cicadas
were winding up time
with a wheezing
of rusty springs
of ratchets
of keyways
and wheels

winding up what was dead here
dead as a photograph
of all of us
the fire and the diamond studs
nobody stooped for
and the horses waiting
as if carved out of wood
and only the wooden horse
rocking

and the gray
gauze trails of moss
animate on the wind
none of us felt
swaying over the house
that was going
under our gaze
in a sleepwalk of flame

THE DICE

•   •

So this
is how
you occupy
ivory space
each centered
assuredly
there

the ayes have it
ambs aces

or think
of two figures
in a field
when each has
a square of snow
and each stands on it
like a tin soldier

otherwise
and elsewhere
the sky merges
into the snow

but we
isolate
stand
on our own stand

on our plinth
on the block
top surface
of our own
opaque box

nor could we meet
quite
if our shadows
did

nor even be one
if the earth darkened

      •   •
   •   •

It has been proved
on the boulevards
you cannot make plays
without the one

I mean
with only a pair

one imperils

without meaning to
also upholds

take one away
the two break up
without even
a quarrel

call one
duenna
rival

any name
will do

it is
the dot
O of drama

the singular third
a reserve
against silence

   •   •
    •   •

How they met
themselves
in a wood
in a pool
in a dream

and how

fearful

they drew back

"Not us!"

their feet
were already
touching

"Not us!"

No

only
in a wood
in a pool
in a dream

otherwise

only ourselves
for all time
only ourselves

    •   •
      • •
       •

I misunderstand
your meaning

meaning only
the spell
is cast wrong

or is this
the unluckiest
throw of all?

five, yes
but except
I balance myself out
I am odd, alone
with a tale
and no hearers

In this figure
the dance
truly begins

or say
the ways divide

one you claim
is ardent
and active

but the division
between the blocks
is arbitrary

one way
a weaving
through fire

as if thought
could not also be
fire

up then
on the ivory stairs

"Click click"
the tailor
says to himself
in his dreams

a leap
each time

68

your coat tails
coming on after you
like shears

yet your legs
stay neutral

.   . .
 .   . .
   .

They said lucky
who only stayed

not counted out
not huffed
or puffed

but the house
held

or aslant
stood
one elbow
on the wind

they said survived
who were only
still in

secure
secure
on the slippery
ivory

on the ice
by an inch

on the sea
by a plank

on the ledge
by a finger

in the game
by sevens

• •   • •
• •   • •

"I have moved
the earth"
says the warlord
"to build walls"

"there will be no
breaking of bones
within my armor"

the snow stretches
North and South
East and West

beautiful is the power
of the powerful

it has the whole world
in its spell

"Click" say the ivory teeth
"Click" says the trap in the snow
"Click" says the key in the lock

⠒⠒   ⠢⠒

In the moonlight
I mistook the menhirs
for maidens

nine

or I thought
the meeting
fortuitous

or I thought
the cast fortunate

and when they moved
in dance
or seemed to move

coming or seeming to grow
towards me

white figures
with the shadow
behind each

I remained
there
where I was
drawing a line

as you had taught me
with the stick
you had given me

whether they stopped
first
or I fell asleep
first
I do not know

only I awoke
to find myself
covered with rime

and this child also
alive
and in my arms

This is the very pattern
of the dance

of groves
of constellations

who shall stand
at the center of the one
stands also
at the center
of the other

and must be whirled
twice
into an ecstasy
of all the senses

twice I say
not by proxy
and at the same time
for there is no mirror
no water or polished bronze
to make two sets
of the one dance

indivisible and
double center
either of swords
or wands

of arms
at last
of arms

This cast
is the diminishing
of the dance

fortunate division
seemingly so
the only one

as if the kings
static
in solemn ranks
watching the queens

were hopeful each
not one
owning himself
unpaired

or
as if a soldier
standing among the hosts
before a battle

seeing them wheel in line
as thick as snowflakes

should think

out of such numbers
how will I be noticed?

then let
the odd one out
after ordeal
or casting of the lots
be chosen
to lie in ivory vaults

or say these others
indifferent
cold
be black dots
in the snow

so I lie by her side
enfolded within limbs
not ivory only

so I live lucky in my bones
never so sure alone

Last of the casts
unlucky
too high
too heavy

no echo
of the dance

but hobnails
six in each heel
to print
the morning crust

"Clank clank" says iron

chained men
along the lane

freight cars in drifts
birds freezing
on the wires

the kings again
too sovereign weighed
to scamper into exile

all things immobile
locked in element
might massive masculine

ranked great in space
luckless abiding wrecks
left where they loom
passed with averted eye

LIGHT-YEAR

Winter Solstice

there is a journey in the flabby mushroom pale
and rank smell of the woods the carmelite white
lichen mildew and the sweat of steam out of the deep
alchemic litter layers to origin of beech leaves

slowly you walk against the weather of the week
and no wren sings rocking in balance on a briar
no sunlight blaze marks bark pistachio green
weird on the boughs of one old apple tree

cocoons for fruit Egyptian cloth and bearded seeds
threaded upon the sky only through broken webs
look up to see a cloud pass as in clouded glass
nubs flailing on the air where no hawk rides or rook

all is in layer on layer an absolute of absence
tugging the heavy boots the roots the pull of loam
still sentient still the twitch of one fine needle
pointing you north and north against your will

Spring Equinox

where are the horsemen gone whose crescents here
held half the year to wane in water riding west
through sallow dustfall of the trees did they believe
the light had burrowed where a hazel bends

77

you who still walk the ash cast of these woods the flint
sparks to your ferrule or the gorse is tongued
see only ghost fire yellow green as accidie the catkins
brush on your sleeve the bird's metallic note

is it as lichen on a slate that Midas lingers
or is hermetic change the hidden heat
you stir iron sediment of pools incut in bark
the fingerholds of the December dark belief is over

beside the burnt out embers of a beech bole turning
you see the gleam you see the spent son of the sun returning
but what it is comes back to you from a remembered orient
is the cold color of the mustard weed whose seed is sharper

Summer Solstice

from fire to fire from seed to seed unmade
where twelve sheaves bleeding hardly makes up one
in distant meadows where the drum the frenzied reed
come into woods without a footfall heard

and is it sleep here keeps the birds so still
their nighttime noon green closes into green
tunnels of beech and rhododendron mines
sharp click of water burning dross of flies

not hum of summer or the fretwork sun to show
a breathing or your shadow on the ground
all intricacies pass the glass shows grass
clutching a lighted straw St John St John

search in that green vault where the bone went down
the pale drowned dogrose and the thorny briar
what hare to listen cringes in her form
what bends a stalk or quills the lovely fur

Autumn Equinox

beech trees are black after the rain the larvae keep
their mummery Anubis in the open knots each raindrop dark
of alembic catches the sulphurous sun seen only going through
the wood's long exit custom sets the balances you wait

until the bronze pan greens with verdigris one hedgerow holds
the barrowed bones of badger dragon wolf of Vortigern
Rowena's lips red beyond any sunset in the ripened fruit
of birds singing the thrush is quick the mole turns in his hole

fires into embers you take up a wand and climb
the warrens over Troy the warp of all things clings the weft
frays in the windless still to an idea of beaks remain
the first star says remain these are the lands I light

between one beech bough and another in this circle fix
your free feet on this hill until another turn and autumn equal
the harvest of the husks and in this match of light the light will marry
the line before your birth into the starline

THE DANAIDES

Circe and Her Lovers

all in abundance the poured black of panthers almost the
bloom of damson when in sunlight the quivering fur shades
her flesh also the alert courteousness of gazelles attendant
always to her least wish as if the slightest sigh were a
disturbance in the deep sand shoals of their eyes and the
serpent mesmerized by some erotic spell of its own caressing
endlessly caressing her unsandled foot

a lizard slips over the drawn figures of her book the
great bear a white grub near its paws watches her longingly a
lion plays with her wand

the nakedness of the woman haunch buttock tail ears they play
their colors and moods touch taste scent gaze upon her
autumnal ocelot wintery badger the quick and slow seasons
of beasts few close to comatose watching with morose eyes as
unseen and enduring the brand burns others lit to the fiery
points of their pelts brush nervous by flank and knee or
dance frenzied on their four footprints before her

chameleon sorcery of color the taut fineness of her skin
almost the light green of grapes almost the same translucency
at her breasts and elsewhere olive or cornelian or rose yellow
and changing constantly changing cast shadow cast thoughts cast
memories of these who were once other than this who might still

an owl blinking at her from his perch not caring that a mouse rubs
his silken tufts to please her under the lobe of her ear a
black goat licks her ring

The Danaides

Delilah with the locks, but, Oh, ambiguous
her gaze! Does it show grief
or one more triumph of deceiving?

The camera caught her so. Was Agonistes
for Samson only—who for her Invader
was fraternizing foe, Philistia's Judith?

Within our century one Lowland Jael
despatched her German Siseras with a hatpin—
the sale boche in the bed, the open Bible.

Brought them Valhalla in a lordly bandbox.
That lepidopterous art, a hate of Hecate,
was it allowable for king and country?

Pro Patria perhaps all's fair; *horresco referens.*
She saw the foxes burning in her Flemish farmlands,
gates carried off from Ghent, the sack of Louvain.

Children cried out to her from shattered houses,
their need was bread, instead she brings them vengeance,
these lapidary scalps, this lingering folktale.

Samson's still blind, but who grinds what in Gaza?
The miller's maid with men's hair in her pillow.

Pastoral

At the wood's edge we come on Caliban.
The boy's a roarer,
a drunken lout; wild strawberries
scattered like bloodspots near one hand. The other
clutches his member, center of gravity
in any man. He dreams of riot:
soft cuddled conies
bucking their back legs so,
does' quivering flanks,
the lambtails' frenzy,
all working into air,
soft, seeding, scenting air.

And that high brake of weeds
conceals the gaudy pards of Bacchus stealing
from higher lawns—
the ragged robin clashes with their gold.

It must be said
that this is Spring and everything is wrong
for patient pages. Even the birdsong jars:
"kill-kill!", "kill-kill!" is cried
about the grove. And cannibal as doves they come
the local lovers, your Daphnis, your Aminta;
not coy the boys, not shy their country partners.

For this is Spring, a dream of Caliban,
not easy to be told. Bind up the scythe with flowers,
leave winter seas to batter round her tower.
Where Prospero's king how shall the brute world speak?
She reads all seasons one, remote Miranda.

Sir John by Starlight

Sir John by starlight sleeps deserted
Upon a table at an inn in England:
Within this belly now the stuff of battles
Slips from the white pikes and the rival armies
Rush into ambush.
             In this tun the hops and vineyards
Flow to their seas of amber and vermilion.
White ladies come to blush, to the bed's ending,
Their names remaidened here. From calumny
All seed returns into one fruit—the pomegranate.

A giant weight, a waste of memory
Lies on the board. Beneath the cover
Campfires are out, the suns in setting
Upon a hundred heaths, on foreign cities
Whose siege is on, who drop, soundless, to rubble
Under the ram, the rolling drums, the rain, the scuffle
Of rats' feet in the wainscot in this room.

Silent, by moonlight now, the shroud of snow equates
The winter plain, the lofty hummock,
The Roman features of this dead patrician:
Into a moth-mist now, into November,
The classic landscape and the golden stubble
Where the red fox lies slain, the wicked bluejays
Are hung on staves, their jargon stopped,
Their amorous, quick ways suspended

Woman and the Sea

imagine a whitewashed tower sea holly and a woman
contain in your ears the sound of the wind through
the three openings and doorway of the tower the returning
waves each third second on the pebbles also the rasp
of wind in the sea holly also the wind in the woman's
clothes an austerity of color imagine a gray day
think if you like of isolation or of Ilium
think if you like that she is thinking
she has walked from the bus from the station
think if you like of the lover she has left
or who has left her do not make too much of your thoughts
she will not walk into the sea there is a gravity of situation

whatever the sea may be in a dream a sentimental poem
or a colored print on a wall here it is simply the sea
a consoler perhaps but neither pathos or tragedy
can be set on this stage a consoler by taking away
what even the Greeks would have left us not Sophocles
Aeschylus Euripides everything forced to some point
but the no point is nothing think if you like your own thoughts
that the woman is beautiful in a way that the calm
is not wholly deceptive that the light too is changing
pellucid one moment it is almost opaque at another
what is her lover to this and what are your eyes on the woman

burden the wind say it sighs say the sea holly catches
she must bend to untangle the hooks from the fringe of her dress
rub her leg with her fingers without looking down and afterwards
walk to the tower where she puts out her hands to the stones
she goes once round comes back to the doorway looks in does not enter

think if you like she is blind that she seeks out her cell
think if you like of her life in that small circulation
think of a question to ask ask are the three windows open important

she steps inside the tower and looks out through an opening of slates
and there is an island why an island now and never before
assuredly there is an island or at least a black rock in the water
what should there be there that is not there if we learn of an island

how long does she look at the rock and what thoughts come what thoughts
are beginning a while she comes out but what thoughts there to walk
so straight from the doorway without looking back and behind her
is falling each third second remember a wave of the sea and remember
especially remember I beg you the light and the wind she is walking in